JONATHA

Effective Leadership
Enquiring & Rebuilding

JONATHAN C. CAREY

CAREY PRESS
EQUIPPING ENCOURAGING EMPOWERING

www.ctcnetwork.org

Effective Leadership
Enquiring & Rebuilding

© 2012 by Jonathan C. Carey
All rights reserved.

Published by Carey Press
www.careypress.online

ISBN: 978-0-9854469-9-4

For information on reordering please contact:

Carey Press

www.careypress.online

Or
Your Favorite Bookstore

Effective Leadership
Enquiring & Rebuilding

JONATHAN C. CAREY

This Series Is Dedicated To Emerging Leaders.

TABLE OF CONTENTS

PREFACE

This book was developed to provide, in a workbook form, steps for personal and leadership success. It targets two groups. Firstly, men and women who are in leadership positions globally, as a leadership and life coaching tool. Secondly, believers desiring biblically–based personal development study materials.

The steps are taken from biblical characters reflecting part of their life's quest and challenges. The author, on a limited basis, is available to conduct Effective Leadership related workshops and seminars.

BIBLICAL PERSPECTIVE

Successful personal-leadership developmental steps do flow from the pages of the Bible, but are these steps applicable for believers today? Indeed they are. What then ought we to do with these biblical steps to success?

Perhaps the first step is the creation-maintenance of an environment in our ministries and organizations where they are recognized, taught, and encouraged. Biblical steps to success take place when believers respond in obedience to God's call. They recognize the importance of total obedience, allowing the Holy Spirit to develop their gifts and skills. They carry out their kingdom roles with a deep conviction of God's will and a heightened awareness of the contemporary issues they and their peers face. Above all, they minister as stewards and servants.

We do not stumble across success. Success is a result of deliberate acts. To truly be successful, we must fulfill the will of God for our lives! The Bible teaches that we can be successful only when we are in a right relationship with God. This right relationship is made possible by the death and resurrection of the Lord Jesus Christ and the indwelling presence of the Holy Spirit. This success is maintained by an ongoing, intimate relationship with God reflected in a life of obedience.

INTRODUCTION

Welcome to this study on *Effective Leadership-Enquiring & Rebuilding*. The principles are taken from the life of an Old Testament leader by the name of Nehemiah. The principles are found in the book that bears his name. These principles are timeless and timely for rebuilding and restoring challenges that leaders are facing today.

The major power in the Mideast during the late 600s was Babylon. That area is today occupied by Iraq. Babylon conquered Jerusalem in the year 586 BC and many Jews were taken captive to Babylon to serve as servants and slaves.

In the year 539 BC, the Babylonians were defeated by the Persians. One of Persia's policies was to allow and encourage captive groups to return to their homelands. A great number of Jews embraced this opportunity and returned to Judah. Others stayed and continued their lives in their new homelands of Babylon and Persia. Nehemiah, who had attained a position of prominence as a cupbearer to the king, stayed in Persia. Decades went by and the Jews who remained in their new homelands were firmly rooted, while those who returned to Judah were struggling to rebuild and restore their homeland.

The Book of Nehemiah begins in 445 BC in the city of Susa, capital of Persia, where Nehemiah serves as cupbearer in the royal court.

Throughout the Book of Nehemiah, we see numerous effective leadership principles in the art of enquiring and rebuilding.

Nehemiah wore three hats: he was a *cupbearer*, a *builder*, and a *governor*. In our study, we will view the enquiring & rebuilding principles from his roles as cupbearer and builder. This study provides numerous projects for you to complete.

I highly recommend that you do not rush through the material, but approach it with our step-by-step method. The overall study format will be consistent throughout. The method of study is derived from the acronym STEPS.

Also provided for you is an *Effective Leadership Personal Audit.* This audit serves as an assessment tool and a goal-setting device. The audit should be taken at the conclusion of each section. Let's now take the first step!

STEPS

State the step
Teach the step
Evaluate the step
Practice the step
See the success

PART ONE

The Fine Art of Enquiring
Others, God, Superiors

STEP ONE

Enquiring of Others

"The words of Nehemiah the son of Hachaliah. And it came to pass in the month Chisleu, in the twentieth year, as I was in Shushan the palace, That Hanani, one of my brethren, came, he and [certain] men of Judah; and I asked them concerning the Jews that had escaped, which were left of the captivity, and concerning Jerusalem. And they said unto me, The remnant that are left of the captivity there in the province [are] in great affliction and reproach: the wall of Jerusalem also [is] broken down, and the gates thereof are burned with fire." (Nehemiah 1:2-3)

STATE THE STEP

Effective leaders enquire concerning the welfare of others and respond appropriately

TEACH THE STEP

Nehemiah was serving as a cupbearer to King Artaxerxes when he received the call from the Lord to return to his former homeland and rebuild the walls and restore the gates of Jerusalem.

The role of a cupbearer may seem on the surface a trivial one; however, this was not the case. Nehemiah served as the official taster of drink and food for the king and was highly regarded. Cupbearers were a line of defense for the safety of the king. If someone was trying to poison the king, the cupbearer would give his life as the first taster. It would be safe to say that cupbearers were literally drink and food bodyguards. So along with the prominence attached to the job, there was the constant reminder of the high risk involved. It would take a special temperament type to effectively balance the sway in emotions. Because of the high risk involved, cupbearers were generally eunuchs and lived and worked out of the royal palace. Their devotion was to the pleasing of the king.

Cupbearers were well dressed and exposed to all the pomp and pageantry of the kingdom. They were among a very limited and selected number of servants who had access to the inner courts of the palace. This access allowed for a number of unique opportunities to be realized, among them were the following:

- Exposure to the protocols of the palace
- Forging of an intimate relationship with the king
- Asking of favors for self and others

Many would use their positions purely for personal gain, not so with Nehemiah. He was aware that his position was ordained of God for the benefit of fulfilling a godly purpose. Effective leaders are able to see the big picture as it pertains to the opportunities presented them. The opportunities Nehemiah enjoyed are also provided for those who serve the King of Kings - Jesus Christ. They are exposed to the protocols of the Kingdom of God, have the privilege to develop an intimate relationship with God, and through prayer, needs are presented and met.

Influence

God had positioned Nehemiah (whose name in Hebrew means "comforter or consolation") in a place of influence prior to calling him to his rebuilding and restoring leadership role. It is said that only a king's wife had more influence over the king than his cupbearer. Often the present influences we enjoy will serve us in our future leadership, nation, and kingdom-building roles.

Effective leaders understand that positions they currently hold may very well serve them in completing God's future assignments for their ministries. Therefore effective leaders serve with a spirit of excellence and a keen awareness of the hand of God in the affairs of mankind. Nehemiah understood this and so did other biblical leaders, among them was Joseph (see Genesis 37-50). Joseph in his trek from the pit to the palace was faithful in his duties and eventually rose to the position of prime minister of Egypt and was mightily used of God. Joseph was:

- Sold into slavery by his brothers but remained efficient
- Solicited and falsely accused by his master's wife but remained faithful
- Put in prison but continued to serve in his gifting
- Promoted to prime minister but remained humble
- Consciously aware of God's favor in his life

It's important for you to not lose sight of God's positioning principle as you serve in what may seem an unrelated job or endeavor to your perceived calling. Be faithful where you are and know that all things do indeed work for the good of those who love and serve the Lord (see Romans 8:28). Your position today may very well be the bridge to your future successes.

Effective leaders understand that faith without works results in kingdom-building assignments being unrealized. Therefore they obtain and protect influence by their work ethic and personal integrity. Effective leaders are careful to treasure influence and view influence as a gift from God received because of good stewardship of the opportunities entrusted to them.

Everyone has a measure of influence. Effective leadership may be described as positive influence in motion. Where is your influence and how is it being deployed? Is your influence available to God?

Enquiring of Others

Nehemiah enquires of his brother and countrymen about the state of the Jews and the city. Effective leaders ask the right questions and in the right order. Great questions almost always reveal the truth of a matter. Enquiring allows us to use an effective tool for analyzing a situation. When we enquire of others, their answers furnish us with their perspective on the subject. Their perspective may not always be correct, but it's important to know how those we wish to assist view their situations. As beauty is in the eye of the beholder, so is a perspective.

The central focus of the Book of Nehemiah is an account of the walls and gates being rebuilt and restored, but Nehemiah first asks about the welfare of its inhabitants. Effective leaders are compassionate about people and their needs, and are not simply projects and results orientated.

It's important to note that Jerusalem was a deep concern for all Jews. However Nehemiah keeps the right perspective as it relates to godly concern. The anthem of effective leaders is "people first." It is important for leaders to communicate to those they lead and their target groups who they endeavor to reach that their welfare is of uttermost importance. Enquiring of others in Nehemiah's fashion will help to accomplish this.

The response received by Nehemiah was that the people who returned are in great distress and reproach. We would hope that if we had survived a great deal of trouble that our lives would be back on track with conditions becoming better and not worse. However, sometimes we survive and all we are left with is the hope that better days may be ahead. Problems can dim our sight and cripple our efforts if viewed insurmountable. The people had little hope and needed effective leadership.

The foundation of their religious and social lives was unstable, and others were taking advantage of them. They didn't want others to do for them; they just needed a level playing field, and a proper structure to function from. They needed a leader who could effectively lead them and the rebuilding and restoring process. God always has someone in the wings. Nehemiah was that needed leader. Enquiring of others is one way to bring the need and potential solution to the forefront.

The Response

Distress and Reproach – Their distress was as a result of the conditions of the walls and gates. The walls and city gates represented *security* and *society* for them. City walls provided needed protection from enemies. A city could literally be locked down at times. Even though they had no present enemies they still felt exposed to possible plunder from without and increasing unrest from within. The elderly, dual and single-parent families, the less fortunate, employers and employees, they all felt exposed.

The need and desire to feel secure is universal and sought after with great cost. Cities and individuals invest a great deal of time and talents to achieve this. It is from a place of safety that we better function and grow our communities, families, and careers. We all have experienced moments in time when we felt distressed from the inability to move forward because of undesirable conditions. Jerusalem was a religious city established by God for His children and its very intent as a refuge city of God was being unrealized.

City gates were the hub of activity. They were much more than entry points. City gates served as a place of government and commerce. The business of town leaders, judges, and merchants took place at the various city gates. All efforts of governance and commerce were disjointed and unscrupulous persons had filled the void with their practices of dishonesty and hoarding. The people were distressed because two important pillars of their civic structure were destroyed. It was hardly a city, much less a City of God, without security and society.

Their present conditions opened them to plunder, unrest, reproach, criticism, and insensitive responses from others. This combination can leave a people, as a group, emotionally battered and in utter despair. We all have experienced these conditions to some degree in our personal and corporate lives. The aftermath of both natural and manmade calamities rocks our worlds and leaves us grappling for the strength needed to rebuild and restore. Nehemiah enquired of others and received a call from the Lord to service.

Enquiring of others consists of:

- A godly disposition
- A thoughtful question
- A listening ear
- A compassionate heart
- A discerning spirit
- A willing attitude
- A Spirit-led response

In the immediate study, we will view some biblical responses to the needs of others by leaders. Not all responses are favorable and worth emulating. However we can and should learn from the successes and failures of others.

Effective Leaders Share A Similar Disposition As Nehemiah's

- Nehemiah clearly understood the need

The need was that of restoration. What was lost had to be re-established.

SCRIPTURE TO EXPLORE

What needs are listed in Luke 4:18-19?

_____
_____
_____
_____
_____

According to the above Scripture, where does a leader find the power to meet these needs?

_____
_____
_____
_____
_____

- Nehemiah was concerned about the need

Effective leaders display compassion. Nehemiah connected with the need.

SCRIPTURE TO EXPLORE

Compare Luke 15:20 and Matthew 14:14. What do these verses have in common?

_____
_____
_____
_____
_____

SCRIPTURE TO EXPLORE

Read Acts 8:30. Explain the importance of this verse as it relates to effective leadership.

_____
_____
_____
_____

Digging Deep

Enquiring of the welfare of others is a function of effective leadership. It is impossible to fulfill God's plan and purpose for our lives as it relates to leadership without employing the fine art of enquiring. Our leadership roles will present us with numerous opportunities in this area. Each stage or season of development as leaders may bring new issues that tend to cloud our thinking and hinder us in the area of enquiring, but we must continue to employ this fine art. During your personal study time, look up and list scriptural references for the following topics and complete the exercise. This may seem difficult, but it really is not. You can get help in finding the Scriptures from a Bible concordance, a teacher, pastor, others, or the Internet. Discuss your findings with a friend. You may want to complete the entire exercise with a friend.

• Godly Compassion

1. Scripture Text_____
2. Scripture Text_____
3. Scripture Text_____

a) What is godly compassion?

_____

_____

_____

_____

_____

b) Name two biblical characters who displayed godly compassion:

1. _____

2. _____

c) Why is godly compassion necessary for effective leadership? Give an example.

_____

_____

_____

_____

_____

_____

_____

_____

_____

_____

_____

_____

• Enquiring of Others

4. Scripture Text_____

5. Scripture Text_____

6. Scripture Text_____

a) What is the purpose of enquiring of others?

_____

_____

_____

_____

_____

_____

b) What is active listening? Give a biblical example of active listening.

_____

_____

_____

_____

_____

_____

c) Give a biblical example of how enquiring of others changed a priority.

_____

_____

_____

_____

_____

_____

EVALUATE THE STEP

To evaluate means to look over or inspect and see the good and the bad in something. When we evaluate here, we are attempting to discover how we should view the step of responding to the call we receive. In this evaluation process, you will briefly review some Old Testament leaders and their responses. This evaluation step is designed to assist you in confronting any hindrances that may have a grip on your life and preventing you from properly responding to God's call in a personal or corporate matter. Nehemiah not only enquired of others, but he personally responded to what he heard in a manner that would require his participation in securing the solution to their problem.

RESPONSES

When Nehemiah asked how the Jews and Jerusalem were faring, it revealed a measure of concern and compassion for their welfare. Nehemiah's response to the answers received reveals a high level of commitment to the Lord and his willingness to adjust his life's plans for their benefit. God knows how to stir our hearts and invites us to participate in His work of rebuilding and restoring. However, not all respond like Nehemiah. Many show unconcern for God's plan and purpose or don't plan properly for its fulfillment. Effective leaders accept the burden of service put upon their time, talents, and treasures by God and don't hesitate to begin to seek God for direction. Nehemiah responds positively and begins to prepare his life for service in the call to rebuild and restore.

Leaders respond differently to the calls received and results therefore vary.

• Nehemiah responds to God's invitation. What was the outcome? (Nehemiah 1:1-3)

_____

_____

_____

_____

_____

• Explain a recent invitation you received from God through enquiring of others. What was your response?

_____

_____

_____

_____

• Isaiah responds to God's invitation. What was his response? (Isaiah 6:8)

_____

_____

_____

_____

_____

• How was Isaiah qualified for this assignment?

_____

_____

_____

_____

• Jonah responds to God's invitation. What was the initial outcome? (Jonah 1:1-3)

_____
_____
_____
_____
_____

• Have you ever responded in a similar fashion as Jonah? What was the final result?

_____
_____
_____
_____
_____

• Moses responds to God's invitation. What was the immediate outcome? (Exodus 2:11-14)

_____
_____
_____
_____
_____

• Why do you think Moses had this initial result?

_____
_____
_____
_____
_____

PERSONAL DISCOVERY

• What concerns you the most about enquiring of others?

_____
_____
_____
_____
_____
_____

• What concerns you the most about responding to God's call?

_____
_____
_____
_____
_____
_____

• Name three persons who you feel would give you godly advice in regard to this first step. Make an appointment to see at least one and seek advice or steps to overcome that which most hinders your enquiring of others or responding to God's call.

1. _____

2. _____

3. _____

PRACTICE THE STEP

As we learn and develop steps to success, it is important for us to consistently walk in these steps. By practicing, they become a part of our everyday life and ministry. The step we have just studied is the step of enquiring of others and responding to God's call. How can we practice this step? We practice it daily by evaluating our thoughts and actions. Conduct a daily personal inventory, allowing the Holy Spirit to search the inward parts, revealing what is in your heart. As revelation comes, write down your personal adjustments. This will be accomplished over a period of time.

YOUR PERSONAL ADJUSTMENTS

List ten adjustments that you will make to ensure you live an enquiring life style. Be specific.

1. _____

2. _____

3. _____

4. _____

5. _____

6. _____

7. _____

8. _____

9. _____

10. _____

Practice, Practice, Practice. It is important to practice this exercise of 10 and continually make the necessary adjustments to ensure you continue developing in your enquiring efforts. God is interested in our achieving success in our personal lives and ministry endeavors. Practice this step to success and maximize opportunities and manage challenges that flow into your life and ministry. Practice still makes perfect.

SEE THE SUCCESS

Success may be instant and progressive. True success is responding to the call and challenges we receive in a fashion that is pleasing to God. Success is very much godly results-outcome focused. Today, after a number of years of practicing the step of enquiring of others coupled with the safeguards that I have set up, I find that I am responding to God's voice through the needs of others. The Word of God and the work of the Holy Spirit ensure that the proper discernment is employed. I encourage you to follow through on further developing this step in your personal life and leadership endeavors. You may wish to develop the habit of keeping a journal. Document your steps, pausing at times to reflect, readjust, and ready yourself for future success. Practice the step, see the success.

STEP TWO

Enquiring of God

"And it came to pass, when I heard these words, that I sat down and wept, and mourned [certain] days, and fasted, and prayed before the God of heaven, And said, I beseech thee, O LORD God of heaven, the great and terrible God, that keepeth covenant and mercy for them that love him and observe his commandments: Let thine ear now be attentive, and thine eyes open, that thou mayest hear the prayer of thy servant, which I pray before thee now, day and night, for the children of Israel thy servants, and confess the sins of the children of Israel, which we have sinned against thee: both I and my father's house have sinned. We have dealt very corruptly against thee, and have not kept the commandments, nor the statutes, nor the judgments, which thou commandedst thy servant Moses. Remember, I beseech thee, the word that thou commandedst thy servant Moses, saying, [If] ye transgress, I will scatter you abroad among the nations: But [if] ye turn unto me, and keep my commandments, and do them; though there were of you cast out unto the uttermost part of the heaven, [yet] will I gather them from thence, and will bring them unto the place that I have chosen to set my name there. Now these [are] thy servants and thy people, whom thou hast redeemed by thy great power, and by thy strong hand. O Lord, I beseech thee, let now thine ear be attentive to the prayer of thy servant, and to the prayer of thy servants, who desire to fear thy name: and prosper, I pray thee, thy servant this day, and grant him mercy in the sight of this man. For I was the king's cupbearer." (Nehemiah 1:4-11)

STATE THE STEP

Effective leaders faced with challenges enquire of God first using correct protocol

TEACH THE STEP

Like Nehemiah, we face varying challenges and experience different levels of related anxiety. He was brokenhearted and would weep over the ruins of the walls and gates and the distress of its inhabitants, but he maintained a level head, knowing that God's plan and favor must be firstly secured before any action on his part. Effective leadership has the ability to balance emotions with composure. To make matters worse, Jerusalem was some 800 miles away and Nehemiah was employed by an unbeliever, so distance and favor from his employer were two immediate concerns.

We all display varying responses when something negative comes to our attention. In The Bahamas, my homeland, there was a popular television talk show called "Immediate Response." It gained its popularity through highlighting the immediate responses of the citizenry to the social and political happenings in the nation.

It is easy to say let's roll up our sleeves and do something, claiming that anything is better than nothing done. It is easy to start blaming others or changing a system of operation when there is a breakdown of any sort. It is easy to feel there must be an immediate response on our part to show solidarity. Nehemiah didn't do any of these and he didn't put pen to paper and resign or ask for a leave of absence from his job either. His immediate response was to stay put. Nehemiah was wise enough to not make any hasty or rash decisions, but to take the matter to God in prayer. Effective leaders consider first the spiritual implications of a matter. Here are his steps to success.

His response – And it came to pass, when I heard these words, that I sat down and wept, and mourned [certain] days, and fasted, and prayed before the God of heaven. (Nehemiah 1:4)

Nehemiah *mourned, fasted, and prayed* from the month Chisleu-December to the month Nisan-April; this was a four-month span. It is safe to assume he was waiting for formulation of a sound plan and the right timing to present his proposed undertaking to the king. Effective leadership considers multiple options in planning and tests each one in prayer.

Many leaders have ruined a good undertaking by rushing into it without prayer, watchfulness, and an acute awareness of the importance of timing and preparatory steps for success. God was calling him to rebuild the walls but first he must weep over its ruins, enquire of God through prayer, and wait for godly favor before embarking on implementing any plan. What is your typical first response to hearing troubling news? Nehemiah provides us with a sound method. You don't want to look back over your leadership role and have regrets concerning how you handled situations that arose simply because you acted rationally and not prayerfully. Effective leaders know the importance of prayer. Effective leaders bathe their concerns with prayer and fasting, seeking God's steps to success.

His praise – And said, I beseech thee, O LORD God of heaven, the great and terrible God, that keepeth covenant and mercy for them that love him and observe his commandments. (Nehemiah 1:5)

Nehemiah approaches God with *praise* and acknowledges His worth. God is over and above everything. God is reliable-covenant keeping and responds in mercy to those who love Him and keep His laws. Nehemiah draws this information from his personal experiences of God and also from the writings available to him. Effective leaders understand where ultimate authority is and are quick to acknowledge it and praise God, the holder of it. Effective leaders have a personal working knowledge of God's blessings.

His confession – Let thine ear now be attentive, and thine eyes open, that thou mayest hear the prayer of thy servant, which I pray before thee now, day and night, for the children of Israel thy servants, and confess the sins of the children of Israel, which we have sinned against thee: both I and my father's house have sinned. We have dealt very corruptly against thee, and have not kept the commandments, nor the statutes, nor the judgments, which thou commandedst thy servant Moses. (Nehemiah 1:6-7)

Nehemiah was not just confessing the failures of others. He was confessing his, too. Effective leaders understand and confess their part in the problem. It is easier to point the finger at other leaders and/or those we lead believing the problems are always theirs. We can quickly make a list of their transgressions, but what about ours? God will not, and cannot fully rebuild and restore without true confession. It is important to bring before the Lord your areas of responsibility in failure and unresolved personality or leadership conflicts. Confession comes before our petitions to God and has to be related to God's law and purpose for our lives and leadership roles.

Psalm 51 was written when David, the leader, was confronted by Nathan, the prophet, regarding his sin. As difficult as it is for us as leaders, it is vital we face the sin issues in our lives. When we do, penitence becomes the working of godly sorrow that brings us to the place of forgiveness of sin, deliverance from our sin, and a release to serve God in our calling. Psalm 51 is worth studying as a plan for leadership restoration.

His claiming of the promise – Remember, I beseech thee, the word that thou commandedst thy servant Moses, saying, [If] ye transgress, I will scatter you abroad among the nations: But [if] ye turn unto me, and keep my commandments, and do them; though there were of you cast out unto the uttermost part of the heaven, [yet] will I gather them from thence, and will bring them unto the place that I have chosen to set my name there. (Nehemiah 1:8-9)

Nehemiah prayed back to God His Word. He quoted from Leviticus 26 and Deuteronomy 30. He acknowledged that the promise of God was *two-fold* and the first part had happened as God said. They had disobeyed and were taken into a foreign land. Effective leaders are able to connect what they and their organizations are experiencing to the covenant promises of God, not only the favorable parts but all parts. Nehemiah was now praying the second part of the promise. He was saying, Lord you brought us back and promised to protect us. That part of the promise was still unfulfilled. There are seasons in our leadership roles when we simply must be satisfied to just pray God's promises, having no other personal or corporate desires than the fulfillment of His Word. This was the immediate scope of Nehemiah's focus. Jesus stated to Satan that we must live by every word that comes out of God's mouth (see Matthew 4:4). Jesus lived out what the Word of God spoke of Him, and we ought to follow this example and live out God's plan for our lives and the ministry entrusted to us. Effective leaders know how to pray back to the Father, His Word, and will for their life and ministry.

His petition – Now these [are] thy servants and thy people, whom thou hast redeemed by thy great power, and by thy strong hand. O Lord, I beseech thee, let now thine ear be attentive to the prayer of thy servant, and to the prayer of thy servants, who desire to fear thy name: and prosper, I pray thee, thy servant this day, and grant him mercy in the sight of this man. For I was the king's cupbearer. (Nehemiah 1:10-11)

Nehemiah finally brings his petition before the Lord, and it was a bold one. He asked God to make him successful. He wanted success in his life and the upcoming task, and was not afraid to ask for it. He had found success in his present role as cupbearer but now he was being stretched and other factors were involved.

He needed success outside the parameters of the palace. Nehemiah was facing new circumstances, and different challenges. It's important to know where we are in our leadership journey and understand the potential risks ahead and articulate our petitions to the Lord with this knowledge factored into our petitions. The gifts of the Holy Spirit functioning in our lives will assist with this. How have you been asking for a successful life and ministry?

Nehemiah realizes that in order to fulfill purpose, he needed the favor of those in authority over his life, namely God and the king. Nehemiah recognizes that influence is a key to his success. The success he asked for was the realization of the fulfillment of God's promise. How do you see success and why do you pursue it? Nehemiah displayed the proper balance between prayer and labor. As leaders we are to pray but also to plan and work. Prayer that is productive includes the theme:
"Lord I am available. Send me."
Are you truly available to the Lord as a leader? Are you willing and prepared to leave the comfort of your palace and serve the purpose of God in a different set of circumstances and challenges?

Complete the following study on enquiring of God.

Effective Leaders Share A Similar Disposition As Nehemiah's

- Nehemiah clearly understood the need to enquire of God.

God is supreme and His covenant is unchangeable.

SCRIPTURE TO EXPLORE

What conditions existed in 2 Chronicles 7:14?

_____

_____

_____

_____

_____

According to the above Scripture, what would God promise to do, and do you think this still holds true for us today?

_____

_____

_____

_____

_____

- Nehemiah clearly understood the protocol of approaching God.

Effective leaders know how to enquire of God through prayer.

SCRIPTURE TO EXPLORE

Compare Nehemiah 1:1-11 and Matthew 6:9-13. What do these verses have in common?

_____

_____

_____

_____

_____

_____

_____

_____

_____

_____

SCRIPTURE TO EXPLORE

Exodus 3:11, 13. Why do you think Moses asked these questions?

_____

_____

_____

_____

_____

_____

_____

_____

_____

Digging Deep

Enquiring of God is a function of effective leadership. It is impossible to fulfill God's plan and purpose for our lives as it relates to leadership without employing the fine art of enquiring. Our leadership roles will present us with numerous opportunities in this area. Each stage or season of development as leaders may bring new issues that tend to cloud our thinking and hinder us in the area of enquiring, but we must continue to employ the fine art of enquiring of God. During your personal study time, look up the scriptural references for the following topics and complete the exercise. Discuss your findings with a friend. You may want to complete the entire exercise with a friend.

• **Praise**

1. Psalm 18:3
2. Psalm 99:3-4
3. Ephesians 2:8-9

a) What is the biblical concept of praise?

_____
_____
_____
_____
_____

b) Name two biblical characters who displayed a spirit of praise:

1. _____

2. _____

c) How does one maintain a spirit of praise? Give an example.

_____

_____

_____

_____

_____

_____

• **Confession**

4. Phil 3:13, 14
5. 1 John 1:9
6. Psalm 51

a) Why is confession important for leaders?

_____

_____

_____

_____

_____

b) Name a leader in the Bible who confessed his faults and needs in prayer. Fully describe the event.

_____

_____

_____

_____

_____

c) Is confession to others ever a liability in leadership? Support your answer.

_____

_____

_____

_____

_____

EVALUATE THE STEP

To evaluate means to look over or inspect and see the good and the bad in something. When we evaluate here, we are attempting to discover how we should view the step of enquiring of God. In this evaluation process, you will briefly review principles of prayer and fasting. This evaluation step is designed to assist you in confronting any hindrances that may have a grip on your life and is preventing you from properly enquiring of God.

PRAYER AND FASTING

When Nehemiah asked how the Jews and Jerusalem were fairing, it revealed a measure of concern and compassion for their welfare. Nehemiah's response to the answers received reveals a high level of commitment to the Lord and his willingness to adjust his life's plans for their benefit. Nehemiah displayed the importance of prayer and fasting by not rushing to action.

Prayer is communicating with God. It takes different forms; prayer is talking with God and God talking with us.

• Jesus is our greatest model of prayer. What things did prayer take priority over? (John 4:31-32)

_____
_____
_____
_____
_____

• Prayer accompanied any event of importance in Jesus's life. Read the following Scriptures and list the events and their significance.

1. Luke 3:21-23_____
2. Luke 6:12-13_____
3. Luke 2:32_____
4. Luke 24:30-31_____
5. Luke 24:50-53_____

Fasting is important to the effective leader because it is one of the things that approve us as ministers of God (2 Corinthians 6:3-10). Fasting is withdrawing from food and/or drink and investing quality time in prayer.

• Persons fast for a number of reasons. Read the following Scriptures and state why each person fasted.

1. Genesis 24:33_____
2. Exodus 40_____
3. 1 Samuel 31_____
4. Acts 9_____
5. Acts 10_____

PERSONAL DISCOVERY

• What concerns you the most about enquiring of God?

_____
_____
_____
_____
_____
_____

• Which aspect of enquiring of God is most difficult for you and why?

_____
_____
_____
_____
_____
_____

• Name three persons who you feel would give you godly advice in regard to this second step. Make an appointment to see at least one and seek advice or steps to overcome that which most hinders your enquiring of God.

1. _____

2. _____

3. _____

PRACTICE THE STEP

As we learn and develop steps to success, it is important for us to walk in these steps. By practicing, they become a part of our everyday life and ministry. The step we have just studied is the step of enquiring of God. How can we practice this step? We practice it daily by evaluating our thoughts and actions. Conduct a daily personal inventory, allowing the Holy Spirit to search the inward parts, revealing what is in your heart. As revelation comes, write down your personal adjustments. This will be accomplished over a period of time.

YOUR PERSONAL ADJUSTMENTS

List ten adjustments that you will make to ensure you live an enquiring life style. Be specific.

1. _____

2. _____

3. _____

4. _____

5. _____

6. _____

7. _____

8. _____

9. _____

10. _____

Practice, Practice, Practice. It is important to practice this exercise of 10 and continually make the necessary adjustments to ensure you continue developing in your enquiring efforts. God is interested in us having longevity in our personal lives and ministry endeavors. Practice this step to success and maximize opportunities and manage challenges that flow into your life and ministry. Practice still makes perfect.

SEE THE SUCCESS

Success may be instant and progressive. True success is derived from facing the seasons of our lives God's way. Enquiring of God sets the stage for a productive endeavor. I encourage you to observe others in ministry as they model the prayerful lifestyle of Jesus Christ. Don't be afraid to glean from effective leaders. Prayer is a leader's lifeline. I encourage you to follow through on further developing this step in your personal life and leadership endeavors. You may wish to develop the habit of keeping a journal. Document your steps, pausing at times to reflect, readjust, and ready yourself for future success. Practice the step, see the success.

STEP THREE

Enquiring of Superiors

"And it came to pass in the month Nisan, in the twentieth year of Artaxerxes the king, *that* wine *was* before him: and I took up the wine, and gave *it* unto the king. Now I had not been *beforetime* sad in his presence. Wherefore the king said unto me, Why *is* thy countenance sad, seeing thou *art* not sick? this *is* nothing *else* but sorrow of heart. Then I was very sore afraid, And said unto the king, Let the king live forever: why should not my countenance be sad, when the city, the place of my fathers' sepulchres, *lieth* waste, and the gates thereof are consumed with fire? Then the king said unto me, For what dost thou make request? So I prayed to the God of heaven. And I said unto the king, If it please the king, and if thy servant have found favour in thy sight, that thou wouldest send me unto Judah, unto the city of my fathers' sepulchres, that I may build it. And the king said unto me, (the queen also sitting by him,) For how long shall thy journey be? and when wilt thou return? So it pleased the king to send me; and I set him a time. Moreover I said unto the king, If it please the king, let letters be given me to the governors beyond the river, that they may convey me over till I come into Judah; And a letter unto Asaph the keeper of the king's forest, that he may give me timber to make beams for the gates of the palace which *appertained* to the house, and for the wall of the city, and for the house that I shall enter into. And the king granted me, according to the good hand of my God upon me." (Nehemiah 2:1-8)

STATE THE STEP

Effective leaders know how to enquire of superiors using correct protocol

TEACH THE STEP

Like Nehemiah, many of us have immediate superiors with varying personalities and demands. We strive to develop as individuals and still maintain accountability toward our superiors. At times, this may become difficult as our heartfelt burdens raise to the surface. Nehemiah had maintained the proper balance between work and personal issues but now the time had arrived to enquire of his boss, the king.

For four months, Nehemiah had been praying and fasting and waiting for the right time to express his need to his superior. Successful leaders, among other qualities, have a keen sense of timing in approaching superiors. I believe Nehemiah had a great work ethic and this served him well when he was asked by the king the reason for his sadness. Servants who were sad in the presence of the king were normally put to death. Talk about job decorum, that's a high standard, but because of Nehemiah's sterling performance record this was not his fate.

I believe as one is efficient on his or her job, fictitious markers or tokens are earned. Markers and tokens represent the level of good standing with the superior and the number of them indicates the amount of grace extended when failure happens or favor is sought. I believe Nehemiah had two pocket's full. Many years ago, I felt the call of God to fulltime ministry, left my employment, and after a few months realized I had moved prematurely.

I was prepared to commence job seeking when my former superior informed me that he had held my job open in the event I wished to return. He was a fellow Christian who knew it was just a matter of time before I would leave again, but I had enough markers. Nehemiah had two pocket's full and worked for an unbeliever. How full are your pockets? As we proceed in studying this step, it would be wise to think of your present employee-employer-superior situation.

His moment – And it came to pass in the month Nisan, in the twentieth year of Artaxerxes the king, *that* wine *was* before him: and I took up the wine, and gave *it* unto the king. Now I had not been *beforetime* sad in his presence. Wherefore the king said unto me, Why *is* thy countenance sad, seeing thou *art* not sick? this *is* nothing *else* but sorrow of heart. Then I was very sore afraid. (Nehemiah 2:1-2)

An Unguarded Moment

Nehemiah was serving the king as usual and was able to conceal his sadness for four months. For some reason, on this occasion it became visible. Often leaders are able to compartmentalize the various issues and challenges they face, but on this day the budding leader could not. Perhaps this was the Lord's doing to bring it to a head, allowing Nehemiah the opportunity to express his vision and garner the support needed. God's ways are not always ours and at times it takes as much faith to *display weakness* as it does to *show strength*.

The king knew Nehemiah was not sick simply because he was the taster and was performing his duties. The king also acknowledged that Nehemiah had a perfect record as far as decorum goes. He'd never before displayed sadness in his presence. There is a first for everything.

When confronted, Nehemiah was afraid. Wow, a leader who admits his human weaknesses. It's refreshing when you meet leaders who are not afraid to admit their weaknesses. Many hide them and never come across to those they lead as genuine. It's amazing that no matter how prepared you are through prayer and proper planning that at the moment of truth there is a measure of fear. Nehemiah clearly understood the possible ramifications of being sad in the king's presence, but this was also a defining moment because he knew that "the king's heart is like channels of water in the hand of the Lord, and He (God) turns it where He wishes." (Proverbs 21:1)

God Holds The Hearts

It does not matter if your superior is a believer or not, God has his heart in His hand. We all become fearful when approaching superiors or facing possible unpleasant circumstances. Our hearts skip a beat and our knees buckle as we ponder how in the world will this turn out. Often we are emotionally paralyzed and unable to face our situation, but the Lord can steer the heart of your superior for His glory and your benefit. Your superior's heart is in the hand of the Lord. This is a reassuring truth that helps us keep everything in proper perspective. Initial fear may grip us, but unwavering trust in God and His attributes will give the resolve necessary to face the challenge of the moment in a God-honoring manner.

God At Times Hardens Hearts

We all wish that the hearts of our superiors will be softened by the Lord and steered in our desired direction. However, at times, the Lord will temporally harden the heart of the king. An example of this is found in the Book of Exodus and centers on the Old Testament leader, Moses. Moses received a visitation from God and was instructed to return to Egypt and demand of Pharaoh that he release the children of Israel from captivity. Pharaoh refuses on a number of occasions and in Exodus 11:10 we are told it is because the Lord hardened his heart. One may ask why the Lord would harden the heart of a superior toward me. There may be a number of reasons. In the case of Moses, the Lord wanted to show Himself strong and vindicate as the children of Israel suffered through a series of plagues He would visit upon the land.

In Exodus 12:30-36 we find that the Lord also wanted the children of Israel to leave the land with wealth. When the heart of our superiors is hardened, we need to consider at least two things. Firstly, the vindicating process the Lord employs on our behalf. Secondly, our financial needs. Perhaps we are to remain until we have saved the needed resources for a new venture. Many have left prematurely and failed in the desert heat of the transitional phase. If the heart of your superior is hardened toward you, it would be wise to seek the Lord for the reasons why.

Nehemiah knew God had to work through the heart of the king if he was going to be in position to rebuild the walls and repair the gates. There is value in having a spirit of excellence on the job, a heart after God, and an understanding of His sovereign ways. Nehemiah:

- Modeled excellence
- Prayed for success
- Knew God was his ultimate superior

His request – And said unto the king, Let the king live forever: why should not my countenance be sad, when the city, the place of my fathers' sepulchres, *lieth* waste, and the gates thereof are consumed with fire? Then the king said unto me, For what dost thou make request? So I prayed to the God of heaven. And I said unto the king, If it please the king, and if thy servant have found favour in thy sight, that thou wouldest send me unto Judah, unto the city of my fathers' sepulchres, that I may build it. (Nehemiah 2:3-5)

Nehemiah as an effective leader shared the need of the group first. He was careful to give the reason for his sadness in a language and manner that the king may appreciate. As a monarch, the king knew the importance of a fortified city and citizenry morale. The heart of the king was in the hand of the Lord, so the king asked what Nehemiah wanted. What do you do when someone with the ability to grant you anything asks what you want? The moment had arrived for Nehemiah and perhaps he had rehearsed this moment over in his head a thousand times. However he displayed a powerful trait. He prayed on his feet in a defining moment. He wanted God to grant him any last-minute instructions or the wisdom to properly respond. He asks for the king's blessing to go rebuild the city walls and gates. He states, if it pleases you and if I have favor in your sight because of my work ethic, send me to where my heart is at this present time.

Nehemiah's superior was now left to ponder at least three things. Firstly, do what pleases you. It's my burden but your pleasure. Nehemiah carried the burden of the mission, but immediate success was linked to the king's pleasure. Secondly, review my job performance and lastly send me to rebuild. Nehemiah was in fact saying, I want you to consider sending me, not merely allowing me to go. Nehemiah understood delegated authority. He wanted not only to go with his superior's blessing but bidding. This is remarkable, an unbelieving superior sending Nehemiah to rebuild and restore God's city.

His dialogue – And the king said unto me, (the queen also sitting by him,) For how long shall thy journey be, and when wilt thou return? So it pleased the king to send me; and I set him a time. Moreover I said unto the king, If it please the king, let letters be given me to the governors beyond the river, that they may convey me over till I come into Judah; And a letter unto Asaph the keeper of the king's forest, that he may give me timber to make beams for the gates of the palace which *appertained* to the house, and for the wall of the city, and for the house that I shall enter into. And the king granted me, according to the good hand of my God upon me. (Nehemiah 2:6-8)

Nehemiah enquired of the king and waited for his reply. The king's reply quickly came. The Scripture points out that the queen was sitting by him. Queen translated in the Hebrew implies a close intimate friend. They were not only husband and wife but close friends. Perhaps he waited for her input before making his decision.

Many years back, I was employed as a civil servant and asked to develop a public school for at-risk youth. The school, when started, was lodged in a number of temporary buildings that we always seemed to be politely asked to vacate. I decided to approach a wealthy gentleman in the community to garner his support for the construction of a permanent facility, and after two years it appeared he would solely construct it.

Prior to the commencement dated for construction, I made a calculated error in taking a high-ranking government official to meet him. I sat shocked as the purpose for the facility was altered by the government official and was soundly rejected by the wealthy gentleman. The plug was pulled on the entire construction project. I left dejected to say the least.
After a season of prayer, my wife encouraged me to ask for another audience and attend by myself. It was granted, and the gentleman's wife was in attendance. The heart of the king is in the hand of the Lord and He sometimes shapes it through the queen. The facility was built and is still to this day being used for its intended purpose.

Notice the following from the King's response:

- **The king wanted to know when Nehemiah would return as he was a trusted employee.** Nehemiah asked the king to send him so the king expected he would return. The king valued Nehemiah's service in the royal palace. This is not so of all accountable relationships. There are some persons who employers wish would leave and never return. It is important for Christian employees to understand the value of sound work ethics. There is also another principle in play here. It's the principle of authority. You return to the one who sends you. Often we receive a mandate and instructions from the Lord for the ministries we are connected to. It is important to remember the importance of returning to the Lord through our superiors who would have sent us out. Protection and support is connected to your covering.

- **The king wanted a timeline for the project. Effective leaders always have a plan**. It is better to have a plan and adjust it than have no plan at all. How can you effectively enquire of a superior without a plan? Your superior will send you and expect you to have a well-thought-out plan. It is not a lack of faith to have a plan of action. A plan determines your timeline. We have the personal responsibility to develop as effective leaders in the area of planning. Successful persons in all areas of society become frustrated when those they interact with don't have a plan of action for their endeavors. Many noble endeavors have failed for a lack of adequate planning.

- **Nehemiah asks for letters for permission to travel and acquire needed materials for the undertaking**. If he was being sent by the king, then he ought to embrace the opportunity to be well fitted for the rebuilding and restoring project. Authority and an escort for travel were important. Nehemiah knew there would be opposition to his quest, but he was now on the king's business and could say, read the letter. Effective leaders possess forward thinking and gather the needed tools for any undertaking. The letter for timber was secured to not only build the walls but a house for Nehemiah. He asked for it up front. Can you imagine the talk if Nehemiah had taken materials allocated for the walls and then built his house with them? It's important to state upfront your agenda. Effective leaders don't have a hidden agenda. Nehemiah could now provide for others and himself with the full support and approval of his superior. Many leaders have crippled or ruined their leadership influence by misuse of assets. Often this was not intentional but developed because personal needs were not communicated and accounted for at the beginning of the process of a project or ministry's development. If a leader is not comfortable with stating personal needs, it will then be vital to have a system in place that accomplishes this.

Complete the following study on enquiring of superiors

Effective Leaders Share A Similar Disposition As Nehemiah's

- Nehemiah clearly understood that a spirit of excellence on the job and favor go hand in hand.

Effective leaders embrace opportunities for planning and operate in wisdom.

SCRIPTURE TO EXPLORE

What admonition is given in Proverbs 6:6-11?

_____
_____
_____
_____
_____

According to the above Scripture, what should be a leader's attitude toward planning and what are the benefits of self-motivation?

_____
_____
_____
_____
_____

- Nehemiah clearly understood the protocol of approaching a superior.

Effective leaders know why it's important to respect superiors. It is God's will and leads to success.

SCRIPTURE TO EXPLORE

Compare 1 Peter 2:13-17 and 1Timothy 2:1-2. What are the underlining success principles seen in these Scriptures?

_____
_____
_____
_____
_____
_____
_____
_____
_____
_____
_____

Digging Deep

Enquiring of superiors is a function of effective leadership. It is impossible to fulfill God's plan and purpose for our lives as it relates to leadership without employing the fine art of enquiring. Our leadership roles will present us with numerous opportunities in this area. Each stage or season of development as leaders may bring new issues that tend to cloud our thinking and hinder us in the area of enquiring, but we must continue to employ the fine art of enquiring of superiors. During your personal study time, look up the scriptural references for the following topics and complete the exercise. Discuss your findings with a friend. You may want to complete the entire exercise with a friend.

• Planning

1. Habakkuk 2:2
2. Luke 6:48
3. Romans 9: 21

a) What is the biblical concept of planning?

_____
_____
_____
_____
_____

b) Name two biblical characters who articulated their vision through proper planning:

1. _____

2. _____

c) Why is proper planning important to effective leadership? Give an example.

_____
_____
_____
_____
_____
_____
_____
_____

• Submission

4. Luke 22:42
5. 1 Corinthians 16:7
6. Joshua 1:16

a) Why is submission to delegated authority important for leaders?

_____

_____

_____

_____

_____

_____

b) Name a leader in the Bible who was totally submitted to his or her superior. Give a supporting example.

_____

_____

_____

_____

_____

c) Is submission to authority ever a liability in leadership? Support your answer.

_____

_____

_____

_____

_____

_____

EVALUATE THE STEP

To evaluate means to look over or inspect and see the good and the bad in something. When we evaluate here, we are attempting to discover how we should view the step of enquiring of superiors. In this evaluation process, you will briefly review some principles of submission to superiors. This evaluation step is designed to assist you in confronting any hindrances that may have a grip on your life and are preventing you from properly enquiring of superiors.

When Nehemiah enquired of the king, he fully understood his position as a servant leader. His respect for his boss and humbleness was evident in his enquiring style. Complete the following.

• Discuss what Paul says about submission in Ephesians 5:21-6:9.

_____

_____

_____

_____

_____

_____

_____

_____

_____

• Explain Romans 15:7 in the light of how it may relates to leaders accepting other leaders.

_____

_____

_____

_____

• Caleb was a senior leader who asked God for a mountain. Joshua 14:1-15 gives a brief account. What do you think sustained Caleb in those years of waiting and allowed him to stay submissive to Joshua?

_____

_____

_____

_____

_____

PERSONAL DISCOVERY

• What concerns you the most about enquiring of superiors?

_____
_____
_____
_____
_____
_____

• Which aspect of enquiring of superiors is most difficult for you and why?

_____
_____
_____
_____
_____
_____

• Name three persons who you feel would give you godly advice in regard to this third step. Make an appointment to see at least one and seek advice or steps to overcome that which most hinders you're enquiring of superiors.

1. _____

2. _____

3. _____

PRACTICE THE STEP

As we learn and develop steps to success, it is important for us to walk in these steps. By practicing, they become a part of our everyday life and ministry. The step we have just studied is the step of enquiring of superiors. How can we practice this step? We practice it daily by evaluating our thoughts and actions. Conduct a daily personal inventory, allowing the Holy

Spirit to search the inward parts, revealing what is in your heart. As revelation comes, write down your personal adjustments. This will be accomplished over a period of time.

YOUR PERSONAL ADJUSTMENTS

List ten adjustments that you will make to ensure you live an enquiring life style. Be specific.

1. _____
2. _____
3. _____
4. _____
5. _____
6. _____
7. _____
8. _____
9. _____
10. _____

Practice, Practice, Practice. It is important to practice this exercise of 10 and continually make the necessary adjustments to ensure you continue developing in your enquiring efforts. God is interested in us having longevity in our personal lives and ministry endeavors. Practice this step to success and maximize opportunities and manage challenges that flow into your life and ministry. Practice still makes perfect.

SEE THE SUCCESS

You have now completed the three steps of enquiring for effective leaders. Each step is connected to the others and ought to become a common practice in our leadership roles. As you study leaders in the Bible and elsewhere, look for these steps in their lives and take note of their success. Don't be afraid to glean from effective leaders. The Apostle Paul encouraged others to follow him as he followed Christ. I encourage you to follow through on further developing this step in your personal life and leadership endeavors. You may wish to develop the habit of keeping a journal. Document your steps, pausing at times to reflect, readjust, and ready yourself for future success. Practice the step, see the success. The following Effective Leadership Personal Audit will assist you in determining the changes, if any, that ought to be made to your enquiring skills. It is my prayer that the Lord strengthens you as you strive to fulfill His purpose for your personal life and leadership role.

PART TWO

Effective Leadership
Personal Audit

EFFECTIVE LEADERSHIP PERSONAL AUDIT

Please read each of the following statements. Circle the number that best describes how true each statement is of you.

Enquiring of Others

1. I am committed to an enquiring of others' lifestyle in my personal life and ministry.

1. True
2. More true than false
3. More false than true
4. False

2. The welfare of others is a leadership trait that I consciously try to practice daily.

1. True
2. More true than false
3. More false than true
4. False

3. I am always willing to adjust my life's priorities for the fulfillment of godly purpose.

1. True
2. More true than false
3. More false than true
4. False

4. Compassion is the main motivating factor in my enquiring of others.

1. True
2. More true than false
3. More false than true
4. False

5. I actively listen to the needs of others.
1. True
2. More true than false
3. More false than true
4. False

Enquiring of God

1. I approach God in a similar fashion as Nehemiah.

1. True
2. More true than false
3. More false than true
4. False

2. I understand the value of and practice sound planning.

1. True
2. More true than false
3. More false than true
4. False

3. I can see my faults clearly and always seek forgiveness of God.

1. True
2. More true than false
3. More false than true
4. False

4. I always wait patiently on God's timing for my endeavors.

1. True
2. More true than false
3. More false than true
4. False

5. My leadership role is greatly influenced by my prayer lifestyle.

1. True
2. More true than false
3. More false than true
4. False

Enquiring of Superiors

1. I have earned influence with my superiors through sound work ethics.

1. True
2. More true than false
3. More false than true
4. False

2. I understand the protocol of delegated authority.

1. True
2. More true than false
3. More false than true
4. False

3. I have a covering over my life and ministry.

1. True
2. More true than false
3. More false than true
4. False

4. I always use my influence for godly endeavors.

1. True
2. More true than false
3. More false than true
4. False

5. When appropriate, I always account for my personal needs in ministry endeavors.

1. True
2. More true than false
3. More false than true
4. False

TOTAL YOUR SCORE

Total the numbers and place them in the spaces provided then multiply them by the given number.

True = 1
More true than false = 2
More false than true = 3
False = 4

True_____
More true than false_____
More false than true_____
False_____

Add the numbers together and read the results of your audit.

Total_____

IF YOUR TOTAL SCORE IS:

15-25 The three enquiring skills are engrained in your personal life and leadership role.

26-35 You are practicing the three skills. If your total score is closer to 35, you need to pay more attention to one or more of the skills.

36-45 You need to continue to work on developing all three skills.

46-60 Others probably do not view you as an effective leader. You may want to take some time to rethink your motives for service.

PERSONAL IMPROVEMENT STEPS

The purpose of this exercise is to focus on identifying areas needing improvement and developing a plan for the same.

STEP ONE: List an area where your score is a 3 or 4.

ENQUIRING OF OTHERS

_____

My score is a _____

STEP TWO: Develop a plan for personal improvement. Refer to your personal adjustments list of 10 to draw your information for developing the plan. Refine your list of 10 into five and record it here.

PERSONAL DEVELOPMENT PLAN

1.

2.

3.

4.

5.

_____

_____

_____

_____

_____

_____

_____

_____

_____

_____

_____

_____

_____

_____

_____

PERSONAL IMPROVEMENT STEPS

The purpose of this exercise is to focus on identifying areas needing improvement and developing a plan for the same.

STEP ONE: List an area where your score is a 3 or 4.

ENQUIRING OF GOD

_____

My score is a _____

STEP TWO: Develop a plan for personal improvement. Refer to your personal adjustments list of 10 to draw your information for developing the plan. Refine your list of 10 into five and record it here.

PERSONAL DEVELOPMENT PLAN

1.

2.

3.

4.

5.

_____
_____
_____
_____
_____
_____
_____
_____
_____
_____
_____
_____
_____
_____
_____
_____

PERSONAL IMPROVEMENT STEPS

The purpose of this exercise is to focus on identifying areas needing improvement, and developing a plan for the same.

STEP ONE: List an area where your score is a 3 or 4.

ENQUIRING OF SUPERIORS

_____

My score is a _____

STEP TWO: Develop a plan for personal improvement. Refer to your personal adjustments list of 10 to draw your information for developing the plan. Refine your list of ten into five and record it here.

PERSONAL DEVELOPMENT PLAN

1.

2.

3.

_____
_____
_____
_____
_____
_____
_____
_____
_____
_____
_____
_____
_____

4.

_____
_____
_____
_____
_____
_____
_____
_____
_____
_____
_____
_____
_____

5.

_____
_____
_____
_____
_____
_____
_____
_____
_____
_____
_____
_____
_____
_____

You have now completed your personal development plan. As you begin to implement your plan it will be wise to continually review and seek guidance from the Holy Spirit. Your plan will assist you in moving forward in your walk in the spirit. It is important to strengthen your weak areas and build upon your strengths. This process may be repeated as necessary.

PART THREE

The Fine Art of Rebuilding
Preparation, Process, Problems

STEP FOUR

The Preparation

"So I came to Jerusalem, and was there three days. And I arose in the night, I and some few men with me; neither told I any man what my God had put in my heart to do at Jerusalem: neither was there any beast with me, save the beast that I rode upon. And I went out by night by the gate of the valley, even before the dragon well, and to the dung port, and viewed the walls of Jerusalem, which were broken down, and the gates thereof were consumed with fire. Then I went on to the gate of the fountain, and to the king's pool: but there was no place for the beast that was under me to pass. Then went I up in the night by the brook, and viewed the wall, and turned back, and entered by the gate of the valley, and so returned. And the rulers knew not whither I went, or what I did; neither had I as yet told it to the Jews, nor to the priests, nor to the nobles, nor to the rulers, nor to the rest that did the work. Then said I unto them, Ye see the distress that we are in, how Jerusalem lieth waste, and the gates thereof are burned with fire: come, and let us build up the wall of Jerusalem, that we be no more a reproach. Then I told them of the hand of my God which was good upon me; as also the king's words that he had spoken unto me. And they said, Let us rise up and build. So they strengthened their hands for this good work." (Nehemiah 2: 11-18)

STATE THE STEP

Effective leaders understand the importance of preparatory steps before starting an undertaking

TEACH THE STEP

Nehemiah arrives in Jerusalem some 800 miles from the palace to commence the rebuilding and restoring process. Nehemiah was accompanied by a royal escort, armed with a purpose, and furnished with letters from Artaxerxes. The letters would allow for travel throughout the kingdom and securing of needed materials for the undertaking. Nehemiah had done his homework well, and one would think he was prepared and ready to immediately commence the rebuilding and restoration of the city's walls and gates.

Sizing Up The Situation

So I came to Jerusalem, and was there three days. (Nehemiah 2:11)

Nehemiah didn't immediately move forward in the project. He waited, observed, and sought the Lord for the first three days. He had articulated his broad plan to Artaxerxes, but now he needed definitive steps to success to share with possible stakeholders.

Waited and Observed

Perhaps he spent part of those days getting a feel or pulse for the attitude of the people and the place. Jerusalem would not have been familiar to him and he would have needed to become better acquainted with the place and the mood of its inhabitants. It would have been foolish to commence a project of such a magnitude without first understanding these important factors. He needed their support if the project was to be successful. After all, it was to be a collaborative effort and not one man's dream. Effective leaders are able to gauge the receptiveness of possible stakeholders to a project and fashion their sales pitch accordingly. Effective leaders seek to understand the nature, history, and character of those they wish to lead.

By looking around, effective leaders better understand the possible *apprehensions* and *desires* of their possible teams in respect to an undertaking. The populace, for the greater part, was in despair and would have to be approached with tact. Often it's not only what is said but how one communicates the vision that secures willing corporation. Nehemiah looked around.

Prayed

The Scriptures do not reveal what Nehemiah did those three days, but it would be safe to say he also prayed. Throughout the book of Nehemiah, we come to realize that the success of Nehemiah's public life was due in great part to a prayerful private life. It appears his favorite leadership position was on his knees. He understood that God orders the steps of effective leaders and he sought the Lord for those stepping orders.

When one waits on the Lord and follows His directives, it eliminates wasted steps and the back tracking that hasty actions produce. Haste may result in a merry-go-round experience minus the merry. After three days, Nehemiah has the pulse of the people and God. Nehemiah looked up and received the direction he sought. When one looks up to God in prayer for answers, he or she is also looking within to evaluate personal motives. Looking within before launching a project allows one to keep a proper perspective. Nehemiah knew in his own strength success was impossible and he would need to guard his heart from impending fear. He looked up, and within. Not to frustrate himself, but to reassure himself of God's grace and empowerment.

Evaluating The Situation

I arose in the night, I and some few men with me; neither told I any man what my God had put in my heart to do at

Jerusalem: neither was there any beast with me, save the beast that I rode upon. (Nehemiah 2:12)

After getting the mind of the Lord on the matter, Nehemiah sets out to inspect the walls. He looks forward to the project and its possible difficulties and solutions. Notice the following:

- **He inspects at night** - It was not his intention to draw attention to himself or the project just yet. He wanted to evaluate the situation thoroughly and knew that drawing attention would hinder that objective. The evaluation stage was to be an isolated mission. It was to be free from debate and questioning. His actions were calculated. The presence of a plan does not nullify a faith walk, it confirms.

- **He protected himself** - He took a few men with him for safety reasons. Effective leaders don't throw caution to the wind. Effective leaders factor in safety measures. Employing safety precautions is not a sign of a lack of faith. It is protecting the driving-force leader of the project. Effective leaders operate in a spirit of wisdom. If God had called him to rebuild and restore, he owed it to God and the project to protect himself from unnecessary harm (see Luke 4:30). A leader has a personal responsibility to stay safe in order to complete an assignment.

- **He told no one what God had put in his heart** - There is a time to declare what your mission is, but it's not in the evaluation stage. It's important for leaders to know when to keep a matter and when to disclose it. Many endeavors have failed even before getting off the ground because of premature disclosure. Learn to guard a matter until the appointed time to reveal it. Do your homework first, and often homework is not a group activity for the effective leader.

- **He took no other beast with him but the one he rode on** - This tactic protected him from giving the impression, if found out, that he was on official business. Royal and government officials would have a grand parade when entering a city to conduct business. Nehemiah understood that this was a God assignment and not a public show. Therefore he downplayed the event as much as possible.

Viewing The Site

And I went out by night by the gate of the valley, even before the dragon well, and to the dung port, and viewed the walls of Jerusalem, which were broken down, and the gates thereof were consumed with fire. Then I went on to the gate of the fountain, and to the king's pool: but there was no place for the beast that was under me to pass. Then went I up in the night by the brook, and viewed the wall, and turned back, and entered by the gate of the valley, and so returned. (Nehemiah 2:13-15)

On two occasions, the Scriptures mention viewing the walls. The word "viewing" connotes inspecting. Literally, Nehemiah was probing the site. He was not only looking at the damage but determining as much as possible a rebuilding and restoration strategy. In any endeavor, knowledge is power. He not only probed the ruined walls but the other infrastructure components. The ruin was great, and it reflected the punishment of God upon a rebellious people. Nehemiah also knew that God, faithful to His Word, would want the restoration to be as significant.

Nehemiah was probing as a medical doctor would with a patient. His probing was slow and deliberate. Effective leadership is not always reflected in the lights and glamour but often the methodical viewing, probing work behind the scenes. Effective leaders are faithful behind the scenes and rewarded with success. I believe he would have done the following:

- Evaluated what parts of the overall city's infrastructure needed strengthening. It was not just about rebuilding the walls and restoring the gates as an isolated project. This was to be an exercise in improving (Dragon Well-Incinerator and Dung Port-Sewer System) all related utility services. How many times have you seen in your city one agency repave a road and another agency come right behind and dig it up to lay new water lines? It happens all the time. Nehemiah wanted to avoid mismanagement of resources, including time, and to allow for further expansion. Many times a rebuilding project allows for substantial improvements.

- Determined what types of skilled and unskilled workers were needed. He wanted everyone to be part of the team. There had to be a role for all for it to be a united effort.

- Developed a rough master plan for the project. It's better to present a plan to possible stakeholders and have it adjusted than having no plan to present. A plan breathes an air of confidence.

- Prayed over the ruins. As a man of prayer, it would be safe to say his probing was done in a spirit of prayer, pausing at times to hear and respond to the voice of the Holy Spirit. Whether it's a building project or outreach thrust, effective leaders pray over projects with an ear bent toward the voice of the Holy Spirit.

Nehemiah understood that when preparation meets opportunity, it increases the possibility for success. Nehemiah didn't shrink from his responsibility to prepare and plan well. His example of discipline is remarkable and was rewarded.

In the immediate study we will view some biblical examples of preparation. Not all examples are favorable and worth emulating. However, we can and should learn from the successes and failures of others.

Effective Leaders Share Disposition Similar To Nehemiah's

- Nehemiah clearly understood the importance of preparation.

Preparation is the behind-the-scenes labor often overlooked by budding leaders. There ought to be a preparation time assigned to every godly endeavor.

SCRIPTURE TO EXPLORE

Read Luke 6:47-47. Of the two builders in the parable, one is a thoughtful builder and the other is thoughtless, not considering the possibilities of the future. What lesson can be gleaned here?

_____

_____

_____

_____

_____

SCRIPTURE TO EXPLORE

Read 1 Peter 1:13-16. Explain the importance of these verses as it relates to effective leadership.

_____

_____

_____

_____

_____

Digging Deep

Effective leaders know the importance of proper preparation. The preparation season is vital for success in any endeavor. Our leadership roles will present us with numerous opportunities in this area. Each stage or season of development as leaders may bring new issues that tend to cloud our thinking and hinder us in the area of preparation, but we must continue to employ this fine art. During your personal study time, look up and list scriptural references for the following topics and complete the exercise. This may seem difficult, but it really is not. You can get help in finding the Scriptures from a Bible concordance, a teacher, pastor, others, or the Internet. Discuss your findings with a friend. You may want to complete the entire exercise with a friend.

- **Godly Preparation**

1. Scripture Text_____

2. Scripture Text_____

3. Scripture Text_____

a) What is godly preparation?

_____
_____
_____
_____
_____

b) Name two biblical characters who displayed godly preparation:

1. _____

2. _____

c) Why is godly preparation necessary for effective leadership? Give an example.

_____
_____
_____
_____
_____
_____
_____
_____
_____
_____
_____

• **Godly Wisdom**

4. Scripture Text_____

5. Scripture Text_____

6. Scripture Text_____

a) What is godly wisdom? Give a leadership example.

_____

_____

_____

_____

_____

_____

b) How would a leader receive godly wisdom?

_____

_____

_____

_____

_____

_____

c) Give a biblical example of how godly wisdom was employed in a building endeavor.

_____

_____

_____

_____

_____

_____

EVALUATE THE STEP

To evaluate means to look over or inspect and see the good and the bad in something. When we evaluate here, we are attempting to discover how we should view the step of preparation in our rebuilding and restoring efforts.

This evaluation step is designed to assist you in confronting any hindrances that may have a grip on your life and are preventing you from properly preparing for the assignments given you by the Lord.

PREPARATION

Dictionary.com defines prepare as: to put things or oneself in readiness. Prepare is to gird up or make ready for a journey or work. Preparation is a key factor in our effectiveness as leaders. If we prepare, God will honor that preparation.

Throughout the book of Nehemiah, we observe its main character constantly embracing the opportunity to prepare properly for upcoming undertakings. It is from this prayerful preparation he draws godly courage to move forward in his assignments. He not only knows the value of preparation but seems to relish it.

Effective leaders and successful persons in any field of endeavor complete their homework well and display a high level of proficiency in their work. The step of preparation must not be overlooked by the Christian leader. Faith is the essence of things hoped for (see Hebrews 11:1), and that is precisely the desired outcome of preparation. One prepares to realize success.

Persons prepare differently for the call to leadership and results therefore vary.

• In what three ways did Jesus prepare for ministry? (Mark 1:1-20)

• How did God prepare David to be king? (1 Samuel 17:55-18:9)

• According to (1 Peter 3:3-4), in what ways does God want us to prepare our lives for service?

• Read the book of Esther (Esther 1-10) and answer the following questions:

• What preparation did Esther go through to become queen?

• What is the importance of God's timing in your life and leadership roles?

_____
_____
_____
_____
_____

• What effect did Esther's background have on God's purpose for her life?

_____
_____
_____
_____
_____

• What preparation steps does God take us through?

_____
_____
_____
_____
_____

PERSONAL DISCOVERY

• What concerns you the most about preparation for an undertaking?

_____
_____
_____
_____
_____

• Have you ever failed because of a lack of preparation? Please explain.

_____

_____

_____

_____

_____

_____

• Name three persons who you feel would offer you godly advice in regard to this first step. Make an appointment to see at least one and seek advice or steps to overcome that which most hinders your preparation for success.

1. _____

2. _____

3. _____

PRACTICE THE STEP

As we learn and develop steps to success, it is important for us to consistently walk in these steps. By practicing, they become a part of our everyday life and ministry. The step we have just studied is the step of preparation. How can we practice this step? We practice it daily by evaluating our thoughts and actions. Conduct a daily personal inventory, allowing the Holy Spirit to search the inward parts, revealing what is in your heart. As revelation comes, write down your personal adjustments. This will be accomplished over a period of time.

YOUR PERSONAL ADJUSTMENTS

List ten adjustments that you will make to ensure you properly prepare for upcoming undertakings. Be specific.

1. _____

2. _____

3. _____

4. _____

5. _____

6. _____

7. _____

8. _____

9. _____

10. _____

Practice, Practice, Practice. It is important to practice this exercise of 10 and continually make the necessary adjustments to ensure you continue developing in your preparation efforts. God is interested in our having success in our personal lives and ministry endeavors. Practice this step to success and maximize opportunities and manage challenges that flow into your life and ministry. Practice still makes perfect.

SEE THE SUCCESS

Success is very much the result of a godly process. True success is responding to the call and challenges we receive in a fashion that is pleasing to God. Success is very much godly results-outcome focused. Nehemiah's method of preparation is a fine example of attention to detail and the pursuit of godly success. His example should be emulated by leaders.

The Word of God and the work of the Holy Spirit ensure that the proper discernment is employed in our rebuilding efforts. I encourage you to follow through on further developing this step in your personal life and leadership endeavors. Study the preparation strategies of leaders within and outside the pages of the Bible. Remember, there is always to be a preparation time.

You may wish to develop the habit of keeping a journal. Document your steps, pausing at times to reflect, readjust, and ready yourself for future success. Practice the step, see the success.

STEP FIVE

The Process

Then Eliashib the high priest rose up with his brethren the priests, and they builded the sheep gate; they sanctified it, and set up the doors of it; even unto the tower of Meah they sanctified it, unto the tower of Hananeel. (Nehemiah 3:1)

And next unto them the Tekoites repaired; but their nobles put not their necks to the work of their Lord. (Nehemiah 3:5)

But it came to pass, *that* when Sanballat, and Tobiah, and the Arabians, and the Ammonites, and the Ashdodites, heard that the walls of Jerusalem were made up, *and* that the breaches began to be stopped, then they were very wroth, And conspired all of them together to come *and* to fight against Jerusalem, and to hinder it. Nevertheless we made our prayer unto our God, and set a watch against them day and night, because of them. And Judah said, The strength of the bearers of burdens is decayed, and *there is* much rubbish; so that we are not able to build the wall. And our adversaries said, They shall not know, neither see, till we come in the midst among them, and slay them, and cause the work to cease. And it came to pass, that when the Jews which dwelt by them came, they said unto us ten times, From all places whence ye shall return unto us *they will be upon you*. Therefore set I in the lower places behind the wall, *and* on the higher places, I even set the people after their families with their swords, their spears, and their bows. And I looked, and rose up, and said unto the nobles, and to the rulers, and to the rest of the people, Be not ye afraid of them: remember the Lord, *which is* great and terrible, and fight for your brethren, your sons, and your daughters, your wives, and your houses. And it came to pass, when our enemies heard that it was known unto us, and God had brought their counsel to naught, that we returned all of us to the wall, every one unto his work.

And it came to pass from that time forth, *that* the half of my servants wrought in the work, and the other half of them held both the spears, the shields, and the bows, and the habergeons; and the rulers *were* behind all the house of Judah. They which builded on the wall, and they that bare burdens, with those that laded, *every one* with one of his hands wrought in the work, and with the other *hand* held a weapon. For the builders, every one had his sword girded by his side, and *so* builded.

And he that sounded the trumpet *was* by me. And I said unto the nobles, and to the rulers, and to the rest of the people, The work *is* great and large, and we are separated upon the wall, one far from another. In what place *therefore* ye hear the sound of the trumpet, resort ye thither unto us: our God shall fight for us. So we labored in the work: and half of them held the spears from the rising of the morning till the stars appeared. Likewise at the same time said I unto the people, Let everyone with his servant lodge within Jerusalem, that in the night they may be a guard to us, and labor on the day. So neither I, nor my brethren, nor my servants, nor the men of the guard which followed me, none of us put off our clothes, saving that every one put them off for washing. (Nehemiah 4:7-23)

STATE THE STEP

Effective leaders understand and employ the underlining
principles of a rebuilding process

TEACH THE STEP

Nehemiah completed the preparation for the rebuilding and restoration of the walls and gates and made his sales pitch. It was well received. The moment had arrived for the implementation of the plan. Often at this stage of a project, leaders hope for at least the following:

- Influential stakeholders would lead the way
- Opposition would be minimal
- Overall morale would stay high
- Adjustments would be few and far between

Stakeholders – Then Eliashib the high priest rose up with his brethren the priests, and they builded the sheep gate; they sanctified it, and set up the doors of it; even unto the tower of Meah they sanctified it, unto the tower of Hananeel. (Nehemiah 3:1)

Nehemiah's expectation in this area was realized. Eliashib the high priest and the other priests were the first to respond. Jerusalem was God's city, and God's representatives led the way as the first wave of workers. This was a tangible sign that the message of repentance and restoration was received by the religious community. Nehemiah was leading a rebuilding and restoration project that should have been initiated by the religious leaders. However, they are to be commended for the humility shown and the willingness to not only get onboard but be the first responders. Restoration takes place inwardly first. God works from the inside out.

Nehemiah was an effective leader and it is seen in the way he allows:

- Influential workers to lead the way. Among every group there are official and unofficial leaders. Effective leaders know how to influence the influential and permit them to move a project along.

- The team to have meaningful involvement in the project. Everyone who desired to be a part of the team was allowed (see Nehemiah 3). His preparatory steps were now being put to use. When workers function in areas of skill, interest, and passion, favorable results are quickly seen.

Effective leaders know the value in allowing the strengths of others to be properly employed. Unity is not about just getting a group to work together but also about individuals within the team functioning in their strengths for the betterment of others and the success of the project.

Minimal Opposition – And next unto them the Tekoites repaired; but their nobles put not their necks to the work of their Lord. (Nehemiah 3:5)

Opposition among the stakeholders was minimal. Not much is said about why the nobles of the Tekoites didn't get involved. Perhaps it was selfishness and/or pride. There will always be some who feel they don't need to join a worthy cause. They have allowed pride to darken their view and selfishness to guide their desires. Nehemiah didn't waste valuable time courting them. He went with the committed. It is important not to allow a few to hold back the energy of the many. Now was the time to launch the project, not engage in further dialogue. Effective leaders understand the importance of timing and move in the moment. Effective leaders don't allow minimal opposition to derail a project.

Enormous Opposition – But it came to pass, *that* when Sanballat, and Tobiah, and the Arabians, and the Ammonites, and the Ashdodites, heard that the walls of

Jerusalem were made up, *and* **that the breaches began to be stopped, then they were very wroth, And conspired all of them together to come** *and* **to fight against Jerusalem, and to hinder it. Nevertheless we made our prayer unto our God, and set a watch against them day and night, because of them. (Nehemiah 4:7-9)**

Effective leaders understand that opposition will come to any undertaking. If no one opposes your work, then you ought to rethink your plans, but when opposition resurfaces in the middle of a project, it's time for alarm.

Effective leaders consider carefully the source of opposition and threats. If it's coming from a godly source, they will revisit their strategies and goals and embrace opposition with an open mind.

Effective leaders must have thick skin and be able to handle criticism with grace and boldness. Leadership is not for the faint at heart. The purpose of unwanted and unfounded criticism is to dishearten and demobilize a team and consequently cripple or destroy an undertaking. Nehemiah's opposition was not coming from a godly source and needed to be met with swift action. The welfare of the workers and the integrity of the project were at risk. It was opposition toward God's purpose and His people. Nehemiah's immediate response was to pray and beef up security. He took his need to God and took precautions. His response was both theological and practical.

Affected Morale – And Judah said, The strength of the bearers of burdens is decayed, and *there is* **much rubbish; so that we are not able to build the wall. And our adversaries said, They shall not know, neither see, till we come in the midst among them, and slay them, and cause the work to cease. And it came to pass, that when the Jews which dwelt by them came, they said unto us ten**

times, From all places whence ye shall return unto us they will be upon you. (Nehemiah 4:10-12)

Almost always when a group hears of opposition to their project it affects morale. Discouragement settles in and godly wisdom is needed to get back on track. The above Scripture states that their fellow Jews told them 10 times what their opposition was planning. Let me say that it's important not to surround yourself with negative persons. If you continually listen to them, you will lose heart as a leader and quit moving forward in your project. It is also important not to hang around those who are always in the company of negative persons. The same result will occur. The discouragement of the group was seen in the following:

The strength of the bearers of burdens is decayed.

- **Workers had lost their strength**. They had been working on the walls and gates for some time and the walls were half built. That is always a critical time for any group. The newness of the project had worn off and physical pain and irritations were setting in. Like a marathon runner, they had hit a proverbial wall. Half-way was a challenge in that they had as much ahead as behind but hands and legs were weary.

There is much rubbish.

- **Workers had lost the vision**. The workers could not see any longer the vision of the completed wall because of the rubbish. They were now focusing on the dirt and debris of the worksite. Discouragement will set in when you take your eye off the prize and focus on the discomfort of the process. The rubbish was actually a sign that the old was being replaced with the new. Effective leaders see the success in the process and use it as a rallying point.

So that we are not able to build the wall.

- **Workers had lost their confidence.** The workers had lost the heart to work. Those who had a mind to work were now declaring that the work could not be completed. This occurred at the half-way stage. Perhaps they felt overwhelmed, not by the work alone, but the personal price they were paying to accomplish the project. Some would have left jobs and other responsibilities to build, and with the impending danger, they now felt empty and spent.

They shall not know, neither see, till we come in the midst among them, and slay them, and cause the work to cease.

- **Workers had lost a sense of security**. We all fear danger and despise the notion of not knowing when an attack will occur. Fear depletes our energy and often immobilizes our efforts. They now were concerned about their safety and that of their loved ones. This had a crippling effect on the workers. They found it difficult to work with the thought in the back of their minds of impending danger unannounced.

Renewed Focus – Therefore set I in the lower places behind the wall, *and* on the higher places, I even set the people after their families with their swords, their spears, and their bows. And I looked, and rose up, and said unto the nobles, and to the rulers, and to the rest of the people, Be not ye afraid of them: remember the Lord, *which is* great and terrible, and fight for your brethren, your sons, and your daughters, your wives, and your houses.

And it came to pass, when our enemies heard that it was known unto us, and God had brought their counsel to naught, that we returned all of us to the wall, every one unto his work. (Nehemiah 4:13-15)

Nehemiah had to bring a sense of safety and a renewed commitment to the project. They had come too far to give up now. It is important for leaders to have a plan for refocus. Even without eternal opposition, discouragement will come to a group and effective leaders will analyze and implement a plan of encouragement. Nehemiah stopped the work while he reorganized the people and implemented the revised plan. Nehemiah realized the importance of taking a break from the project. It allowed workers an opportunity to calm themselves, care for, and accept the comfort of family.

Notice the components of Nehemiah's plan:

Therefore set I in the lower places behind the wall, *and* on the higher places, I even set the people after their families with their swords, their spears, and their bows.

- **Families were unified**. The work force was reorganized into family units. This allowed them to watch out for each other as they worked on the walls. They were now united around an expanded goal, building the wall and fortification. Who best to watch your back than a family member?

Be not ye afraid of them: remember the Lord, *which is* great and terrible, and fight for your brethren, your sons, and your daughters, your wives, and your houses.

- **Focus was readjusted**. Nehemiah in essence said this is not about your opposition or your fear. This is about how great God is and your love for your family and what God has blessed you with. Effective leaders will always prompt the team to regain the right focus. Effective leaders don't allow teams to view from the perspective of fear but from the reality of God's empowerment. Teams may at times have to fight to complete a project, but the Lord who calls to the rebuilding vision is more than able to furnish the strength and wisdom needed for the work and preservation.

And it came to pass from that time forth, *that* the half of my servants wrought in the work, and the other half of them held both the spears, the shields, and the bows, and the habergeons; and the rulers *were* behind all the house of Judah.

- **Plan was adjusted**. Safety on the job should never be compromised for efficiency. The adjusted plan might have slowed down the process of rebuilding, but it's better to be safe than sorry. Half worked while half guarded was the new plan and it worked. News got back to the opposition that the workers were back at the job and the workplace was fortified. Nehemiah had turned the tide in his favor and would employ one last strategy.

And he that sounded the trumpet *was* by me. And I said unto the nobles, and to the rulers, and to the rest of the people, The work *is* great and large, and we are separated upon the wall, one far from another. In what place *therefore* ye hear the sound of the trumpet, resort ye thither unto us: our God shall fight for us.

News got back to the opposition that the workers had regained their focus and returned to the project with safety measures in place. Nehemiah used the occasion to employ a unity-building strategy. He developed a rally place.

- **Rallying place identified**. Nehemiah had committed himself to being mobile. His plan was to move among the project and look out for any resemblance of an attack. If it occurred, he would have a trumpet blast blown and everyone would converge to that place. They now had a rally call and a rally place. In the event of an attack, it was one for all and all for one. It's encouraging to know that you have support not only from your immediate family but also from the wider group that you belong to. They had a place to rally to, and the assurance that they would not have to fight alone.

The workforce stayed at the task working and sleeping in Jerusalem and only took off their clothes for washing. Nehemiah wanted to complete the project as speedily as possible. They had recommitted themselves to the project and were poised for success.

Complete the following study on process.

Effective Leaders Share A Similar Disposition As Nehemiah's

- Nehemiah clearly understood the process would produce its unique challenges.

God not only gives a vision, but the wisdom to accomplish it.

SCRIPTURE TO EXPLORE

What conditions existed in Deuteronomy 1:21-32 that led to discouragement?

_____

_____

_____

_____

_____

According to the above Scripture, what would God promise to do, and do you think this still holds true for us today?

_____

_____

_____

_____

_____

- Nehemiah clearly understood opposition to God's work is to be expected.

Effective leaders know how to adjust their plans because of opposition and threats.

SCRIPTURE TO EXPLORE

Compare Isaiah 54:17 and Matthew 16:19. What do these verses have in common?

_____

_____

_____

_____

_____

_____

SCRIPTURE TO EXPLORE

Proverbs 3:5-6. Why do you think author wrote this?

_____

_____

_____

_____

_____

_____

_____

_____

_____

_____

Digging Deep

Understanding the uniqueness of the process is vital for leaders. Each rebuilding and restoration project will have its challenges and potential pitfalls. Understanding the process is a function of effective leadership. It is impossible to fulfill God's plan and purpose for our lives as it relates to leadership without employing the fine art of rebuilding. Our leadership roles will present us with numerous opportunities in this area. Each stage or season of development as leaders may bring new issues that tend to cloud our thinking and hinder us in various areas, but we must continue to employ the fine art of rebuilding. During your personal study time, look up the scriptural references for the following topics and complete the exercise. Discuss your findings with a friend. You may want to complete the entire exercise with a friend.

• Safety

1. Psalm 4:8
2. Psalm 121:4-8
3. Proverbs 18:10

a) What is the biblical concept of safety?

_____
_____
_____
_____
_____

b) Name two biblical characters who trusted completely in God's keeping power:

1. _____

2. _____

c) How does one maintain a trust in God? Give an example.

_____
_____
_____
_____
_____
_____

• Unity

4. Psalms 133:1
5. John 17:11-23
6. 1 Corinthians 1:10

a) Why is unity important for leaders?

_____
_____
_____
_____
_____

b) What steps lead to a group becoming unified? Describe the event.

_____
_____
_____
_____
_____
_____

c) Is unity of believers a witness to unbelievers? Support your answer.

_____
_____
_____
_____
_____
_____

EVALUATE THE STEP

To evaluate means to look over or inspect and see the good and the bad in something. When we evaluate here, we are attempting to discover how we should view the step of the process in rebuilding. This evaluation step is designed to assist you in confronting any hindrances that may have a grip on your life and are preventing you from properly carrying out the process as a leader.

• Jesus is our greatest model of leadership. What was His management style? (Matthew 23:8)

_____
_____
_____
_____
_____

• Jesus had a clear vision and set of goals for His ministry. Read the following Scriptures and list them.

    7. Luke 4:18 _____

    8. Luke 18:31-33 _____

    9. John 17:4,6 _____

PERSONAL DISCOVERY

• What concerns you the most about the rebuilding process?

_____

_____

_____

_____

_____

_____

• Which aspect of the process is most difficult for you and why?

_____

_____

_____

_____

_____

_____

• Name three persons who you feel would give you godly advice in regard to this second step. Make an appointment to see at least one and seek advice or steps to overcome that which most hinders your rebuilding process.

1. _____

2. _____

3. _____

PRACTICE THE STEP

As we learn and develop steps to success, it is important for us to walk in these steps. By practicing, they become a part of our everyday life and ministry. The step we have just studied is the step of the process. How can we practice this step? We practice it daily by evaluating our thoughts and actions. Conduct a daily personal inventory, allowing the Holy Spirit to search the inward parts, revealing what is in your heart. As revelation comes, write down your personal adjustments. This will be accomplished over a period of time.

YOUR PERSONAL ADJUSTMENTS

List ten adjustments that you will make to ensure you live an enquiring life style. Be specific.

1. _____

2. _____

3. _____

4. _____

5. _____

6. _____

7. _____

8. _____

9. _____

10. _____

Practice, Practice, Practice. It is important to practice this exercise of 10 and continually make the necessary adjustments to ensure you continue developing in your enquiring efforts. God is interested in our having longevity in our personal lives and ministry endeavors. Practice this step to success and maximize opportunities and manage challenges that flow into your life and ministry. Practice still makes perfect.

SEE THE SUCCESS

Success may be instant and progressive. True success is derived from facing the seasons of our lives God's way. Every rebuilding process is unique and requires seeking God's directions. I encourage you to observe others in ministry as they model the leadership style of Jesus Christ. Don't be afraid to glean from effective leaders. Flexibility is a must for effective leaders. I encourage you to follow through on further developing this step in your personal life and leadership endeavors. You may wish to develop the habit of keeping a journal. Document your steps, pausing at times to reflect, readjust, and ready yourself for future success. Practice the step, see the success.

STEP SIX

The Problems

"And there was a great cry of the people and of their wives against their brethren the Jews. For there were that said, We, our sons, and our daughters, *are* many: therefore we take up corn *for them*, that we may eat, and live. *Some* also there were that said, We have mortgaged our lands, vineyards, and houses, that we might buy corn, because of the dearth. There were also that said, We have borrowed money for the king's tribute, *and that upon* our lands and vineyards. Yet now our flesh *is* as the flesh of our brethren, our children as their children: and, lo, we bring into bondage our sons and our daughters to be servants, and *some* of our daughters are brought unto bondage *already*: neither *is it* in our power *to redeem them*; for other men have our lands and vineyards. And I was very angry when I heard their cry and these words. Then I consulted with myself, and I rebuked the nobles, and the rulers, and said unto them, Ye exact usury, every one of his brother. And I set a great assembly against them. And I said unto them, We after our ability have redeemed our brethren the Jews, which were sold unto the heathen; and will ye even sell your brethren? or shall they be sold unto us? Then held they their peace, and found nothing *to answer.* Also I said, It *is* not good that ye do: ought ye not to walk in the fear of our God because of the reproach of the heathen our enemies? I likewise, *and* my brethren, and my servants, might exact of them money and corn: I pray you, let us leave off this usury. Restore, I pray you, to them, even this day, their lands, their vineyards, their olive yards, and their houses, also the hundredth *part* of the money, and of the corn, the wine, and the oil, that ye exact of them. Then said they, We will restore *them,* and will require nothing of them; so will we do as thou sayest. Then I called the priests, and took an oath of them, that they should do according to this promise. Also I shook my lap, and said, So God shake out every man from his house, and from his labor, that performeth not this promise, even thus be he shaken out, and emptied. And all the congregation said, Amen, and praised the LORD. And the people did according to this promise." (Nehemiah 5:1-12)

STATE THE STEP

Effective leaders know how to channel anger and challenge

others to reform

TEACH THE STEP

Every rebuilding and restoring project has problems. As an effective leader, Nehemiah prepared well and built with an eye on the welfare of the workers and detail to the work. Nehemiah dealt with the protocols that were his responsibilities and now is faced with a problem outside his scope. Like Nehemiah, many of us have problems arise in our efforts that are not directly related to the work but are off-shoots. These problems may be unaccounted for in our preparation, but if left unsolved, will derail the work. With the normal pressure associated with the project, these off-shoots can try the patience of any leader.

The workers were faced with a money problem. The community leaders had not prepared properly for the influx of workers and there was a drought in the land. Those factors coupled with a spirit of greed had stripped the workers of their ability to take care of their families and financial responsibilities. The workers went on strike. Everything came to a grinding halt and the fiasco angered Nehemiah.

Reasons for the Work Stoppage

"And there was a great cry of the people and of their wives against their brethren the Jews. For there were that said, We, our sons, and our daughters, *are* many: therefore we take up corn *for them*, that we may eat, and live. *Some* also there were that said, We have mortgaged our lands, vineyards, and houses, that we might buy corn, because of the dearth.

There were also that said, We have borrowed money for the king's tribute, *and that upon* our lands and vineyards. (Nehemiah 5:1-4)

There were at least three reasons for the work stoppage:

- Large families didn't have enough food

- Homes and properties were mortgaged by some and still there were needs

- Those heavily in debt were unable to pay back what they owed

These were the three main concerns and it spilled over to the work. It affected morale. What affects people on a personal level will most definitely affect a corporate effort.

Reasons for the Problems

- Famine
- Taxes
- High interest rates

This could have been today's headline news. It is safe to say that the above three reasons are common in almost all societies. However, hidden among the problems is the main reason for the crisis. The community leaders had not obeyed at least one of God's Community Guidelines.

God instructed leaders not to charge interest to fellow Jews (see Exodus 22:25, Deuteronomy 23:19-20). God had promised that He would bless those who followed His instructions. He desired for Israel to be an example of His covenant blessings.

The project assigned to Nehemiah was not just the rebuilding of the walls and repairing of the gates. God was using Nehemiah to bring conformity to His laws from the inside out.

Nehemiah's Corrective Measures

Then I consulted with myself, and I rebuked the nobles, and the rulers, and said unto them, Ye exact usury, every one of his brother. And I set a great assembly against them. And I said unto them, We after our ability have redeemed our brethren the Jews, which were sold unto the heathen; and will ye even sell your brethren? or shall they be sold unto us? Then held they their peace, and found nothing *to answer.*

Also I said, It *is* not good that ye do: ought ye not to walk in the fear of our God because of the reproach of the heathen our enemies? I likewise, *and* my brethren, and my servants, might exact of them money and corn: I pray you, let us leave off this usury. Restore, I pray you, to them, even this day, their lands, their vineyards, their olive yards, and their houses, also the hundredth *part* of the money, and of the corn, the wine, and the oil, that ye exact of them. Then said they, We will restore *them*, and will require nothing of them; so will we do as thou sayest.

Then I called the priests, and took an oath of them, that they should do according to this promise. Also I shook my lap, and said, So God shake out every man from his house, and from his labor, that performeth not this promise, even thus be he shaken out, and emptied. And all the congregation said, Amen, and praised the LORD. And the people did according to this promise. (Nehemiah 5:7-13)

Nehemiah did the following:
- **He consulted and rebuked**. Nehemiah consulted with himself. He was not rash with his response but weighed the matter. Even in his anger he exercised self-control. This is a much-needed virtue for leaders. From a place of calmness, he was ready to approach the offenders. He rebuked the nobles and rulers. He placed the blame

where it was. It's refreshing to see a leader who is not afraid to challenge the establishment when it is powerful but wrong.

- **Three accusations were fired at the nobles and rulers**. First: you have disobeyed God by charging interest to fellow Jews. Second: you are making slaves of God's people, and third: you are causing us to lose our reflection as God's chosen people in the eyes of our neighbors.

The leaders were rebuked and responded positively. Nehemiah was then able to offer corrective measures.

It is impossible to offer and implement corrective measures if no one acknowledges fault.

Notice the following:

- Infractions were stopped (verse 10)
- Restitution was implemented (verse 11)
- A commitment was made before God (verse 12)
- A public warning was given (verse 13)
- Thanksgiving was offered to God (verse 13)

The problems were dealt with in a godly manner and the work resumed. The project was completed in 52 days.

Complete the following study on problems

Effective Leaders Share A Similar Disposition As Nehemiah's

- Nehemiah clearly understood that problems are inevitable in projects.

Effective leaders face problems head-on and understand that problems unresolved will cripple morale and hinder success.

SCRIPTURE TO EXPLORE

What was Joseph's problem in Matthew 1:18-25?

_____

_____

_____

_____

_____

According to the above Scriptures, how did Joseph deal with his problem?

_____

_____

_____

_____

_____

Nehemiah clearly understood the protocol for approaching a problem.

Effective leaders know why it's important to scripturally respond to problems.

SCRIPTURE TO EXPLORE

Matthew 18:15-20 gives us a system for dealing with conflict. Discuss the system.

_____

_____

_____

_____

_____

_____

_____

_____

_____

_____

Digging Deep

Effectively dealing with problems is an acquired art and often takes years to develop. Effective leaders are committed to developing this skill. It is impossible to fulfill God's plan and purpose for our lives as it relates to leadership without resolving personal and corporate problems. Our leadership roles will present us with numerous opportunities in this area. Each stage or season of development as leaders may bring new issues that tend to cloud our thinking and hinder us in the area of problem solving, but we must continue to employ the art. During your personal study time, look up the scriptural references for the following topics and complete the exercise. Discuss your findings with a friend. You may want to complete the entire exercise with a friend.

• **Problems**

Read Genesis 6-8 and answer the following:

a) Why did God ask Noah to build the ark?

_____
_____
_____
_____
_____

b) Name four problems that existed in the world then:

1. _____
2. _____
3. _____
4. _____

c) Why is proper planning important to effective leadership? Give an example.

_____
_____
_____
_____
_____
_____
_____
_____

d) What problems do you think Noah encountered in building the ark?

_____
_____
_____
_____
_____

e) What problems do you think Noah experienced during the voyage?

_____
_____
_____
_____
_____
_____

c) How do you think Noah solved his problems as they related to the building and sailing of the ark?

_____
_____
_____
_____
_____
_____

EVALUATE THE STEP

To evaluate means to look over or inspect and see the good and the bad in something. When we evaluate here, we are attempting to discover how we should view the step of problems. This evaluation step is designed to assist you in confronting any hindrances that may have a grip on your life and are preventing you from properly evaluating and solving project-related problems.

PERSONAL DISCOVERY

• What concerns you the most about facing problems?

_____
_____
_____
_____
_____

• Which aspect of problem solving is most difficult for you, and why?

_____
_____
_____
_____
_____

• Name three persons who you feel would give you godly advice in regard to this third step. Make an appointment to see at least one and seek advice or steps to overcome that which most hinders your problem-solving skills.

1. _____
2. _____
3. _____

PRACTICE THE STEP

As we learn and develop steps to success, it is important for us to walk in these steps. By practicing, they become a part of our everyday life and ministry. The step we have just studied is the step of problems. How can we practice this step? We practice it daily by evaluating our thoughts and actions. Conduct a daily personal inventory, allowing the Holy Spirit to search the inward parts, revealing what is in your heart. As revelation comes, write down your personal adjustments. This will be accomplished over a period of time.

YOUR PERSONAL ADJUSTMENTS

List ten adjustments that you will make to ensure you live an enquiring life style. Be specific.

1. _____
2. _____
3. _____
4. _____
5. _____
6. _____
7. _____
8. _____
9. _____
10. _____

Practice, Practice, Practice. It is important to practice this exercise of 10 and continually make the necessary adjustments to ensure you continue developing in your enquiring efforts. God is interested in our having longevity in our personal lives and ministry endeavors. Practice this step to success and maximize opportunities and manage challenges that flow into your life and ministry. Practice still makes perfect.

SEE THE SUCCESS

You have now completed the three steps of rebuilding for effective leaders. Each step is connected to the others and ought to become a common practice in our leadership roles. As you study leaders in the Bible and elsewhere, look for these steps in their lives and take note of their success. Don't be afraid to glean from effective leaders. The Apostle Paul encouraged others to follow him as he followed Christ (see 1 Corinthians 11:1). I encourage you to continue to review and apply the principles presented in these three steps. They are time tested and will serve you well in your rebuilding efforts.

I encourage you to follow through on further developing these steps in your personal life and leadership endeavors. You may wish to develop the habit of keeping a journal. Document your steps, pausing at times to reflect, readjust, and ready yourself for future success.

Practice the step, see the success. The following Effective Leadership Personal Audit will assist you in determining the changes, if any, that ought to be made to your enquiring skills. It is my prayer that the Lord strengthens you as you strive to fulfill His purpose for your personal life and leadership role.

PART FOUR

Effective Leadership
Personal Audit

EFFECTIVE LEADERSHIP PERSONAL AUDIT

Please read each of the following statements. Circle the number that best describes how true each statement is of you.

The Preparation

1. I am committed to thoroughly evaluating before launching a project.

1. True
2. More true than false
3. More false than true
4. False

2. The inclusion of all stakeholders in a project is a leadership trait that I consciously try to practice.

1. True
2. More true than false
3. More false than true
4. False

3. I always present a rough master plan for a project to my leadership and work teams.

1. True
2. More true than false
3. More false than true
4. False

4. I always protect myself when it appears necessary.

1. True
2. More true than false
3. More false than true
4. False

5. I always keep a project to myself until the appointed time to declare it.

1. True
2. More true than false
3. More false than true
4. False

The Process

1. I approach my rebuilding process in a similar fashion as Nehemiah.

1. True
2. More true than false
3. More false than true
4. False

2. I understand the value of worker safety and always implement sound measures.

1. True
2. More true than false
3. More false than true
4. False

3. I always take steps to maintain unity among my work teams.

1. True
2. More true than false
3. More false than true
4. False

4. I always wait patiently on God's direction in my readjusting efforts.

1. True
2. More true than false
3. More false than true
4. False

5. I have a firm grip on principles for overcoming discouragement.

1. True
2. More true than false
3. More false than true
4. False

The Problems

1. I am not afraid to confront those who take advantage of others.

1. True
2. More true than false
3. More false than true
4. False

2. I always calm myself before confronting others.

1. True
2. More true than false
3. More false than true
4. False

3. I always take personal responsibility for my part in a problem.

1. True
2. More true than false
3. More false than true
4. False

4. I always present possible solutions for project-related problems.

1. True
2. More true than false
3. More false than true
4. False

5. I have the commitment level necessary to lead my team forward after successfully dealing with a problem.

1. True
2. More true than false
3. More false than true
4. False

TOTAL YOUR SCORE

Total the numbers and place them in the spaces provided then multiply them by the given number.

True = 1
More true than false = 2
More false than true = 3
False = 4

True_____
More true than false_____
More false than true_____
False_____

Add the numbers together and read the results of your audit.

Total_____

IF YOUR TOTAL SCORE IS

15-25 The three enquiring skills are engrained in your personal life and leadership role.

26-35 You are practicing the three skills. If your total score is closer to 35, you need to pay more attention to one or more of the skills.

36-45 You need to continue to work on developing all three skills.

46-60 Others probably do not view you as an effective leader. You may want to take some time to rethink your motives for service.

PERSONAL IMPROVEMENT STEPS

The purpose of this exercise is to focus on identifying areas that need improvement and developing a plan for the same.

STEP ONE: List an area where your score is a 3 or 4.

PREPARATION

_____

_____

My score is a ____

STEP TWO: Develop a plan for personal improvement.
Refer to your personal adjustments list of 10 to draw your information for developing the plan. Refine your list of 10 into five and record it here.

PERSONAL DEVELOPMENT PLAN

1.

2.

3.

4.

5.

_____

_____

_____

_____

_____

_____

_____

_____

_____

_____

_____

_____

_____

_____

_____

PERSONAL IMPROVEMENT STEPS

The purpose of this exercise is to focus on identifying areas that need improvement and develop a plan for the same.

STEP ONE: List an area where your score is a 3 or 4.

PROCESS

_____

_____

My score is a ____

STEP TWO: Develop a plan for personal improvement.
Refer to your personal adjustments list of 10 to draw your information for developing the plan. Refine your list of 10 into five and record it here.

PERSONAL DEVELOPMENT PLAN

1.

_____
_____
_____
_____
_____
_____
_____
_____
_____
_____
_____
_____
_____

2.

_____
_____
_____
_____
_____
_____
_____
_____
_____
_____
_____
_____
_____
_____

3.

4.

5.

_____
_____
_____
_____
_____
_____
_____
_____
_____
_____
_____
_____
_____
_____
_____
_____
_____

PERSONAL IMPROVEMENT STEPS

The purpose of this exercise is to focus on identifying areas that need improvement and develop a plan for the same.

STEP ONE: List an area where your score is a 3 or 4.

PROBLEMS

_____

My score is a ____

STEP TWO: Develop a plan for personal improvement.
Refer to your personal adjustments list of 10 to draw your information for developing the plan. Refine your list of 10 into five and record it here.

PERSONAL DEVELOPMENT PLAN

1.

2.

3.

4.

5.

_____

_____

_____

_____

_____

_____

_____

_____

_____

_____

_____

_____

_____

_____

_____

_____

You have now completed your personal development plan. As you begin to implement your plan it will be wise to continually review and seek guidance from the Holy Spirit. Your plan will assist you in moving forward in your walk in the Spirit. It is important to strengthen your weak areas and build upon your strengths. This process may be repeated as necessary.

www.ctcnetwork.org

Who We Are

The CTC Network, is a non-profit 501(c)3 organization that provides consulting, training, and coaching services to community leaders and individuals throughout Florida and The Caribbean.

What We Do

We work with community leaders and individuals desirous of success in any of the following areas:

- Restoring individuals, families, and communities by addressing spiritual, humanitarian and social development concerns.
- Under-Girding educational systems with support, encouragement, and youth preparedness programs.
- Training and Empowering community leaders and entrepreneurs with biblical vision building principles and micro-credit programs.
- Healthcare partnerships with Governments and NGO's throughout the Caribbean.

Where We Are

Jonathan and Shena invite you to invest your prayers, and financial resources with CTC Network to develop effective *Leaders in Florida, and Caribbean Region* who will reach their communities for Christ.

How To Support

<u>World Outreach</u> Ministries serves as our Home Base Office. They serve us administratively in many ways. They handle our mailing lists, online donations, receipting, computer generated reports, and donor relations. Their services allow us to focus on our strengths which are providing consulting, training, and coaching services to community leaders, entrepreneurs, and leadership teams.

<u>For Tax Deductible Gifts</u>:

1. Online Donations for our account –

www.WorldOutreach.org
Click Donate & select Jonathan & Shena Carey #76
(USA & International Cards accepted)

2. Or, Mail Checks to –

World Outreach Ministries
P.O. Box B
Marietta, GA 30061 USA
(designate for Jonathan & Shena Carey #76)

Made in the USA
Columbia, SC
21 October 2017